EVERYTHING
IS A POEM

Text copyright © 2014 J. Patrick Lewis

Illustrations copyright © 2014 Maria Cristina Pritelli

Designed by Rita Marshall

Published in 2014 by Creative Editions

P.O. Box 227, Mankato, MN 56002 USA

Creative Editions is an imprint of The Creative Company

Printed in China

Library of Congress Cataloging-in-Publication Data

Lewis, J. Patrick.

Everything is a poem: the best of J. Patrick Lewis /

by J. Patrick Lewis; illustrated by Maria Cristina Pritelli.

Summary: A delightfully wide-ranging poetry collection

taken from previously published and new works by

American poet J. Patrick Lewis is illustrated by Italian

artist Maria Cristina Pritelli.

ISBN 978-1-56846-240-0

I. Pritelli, Maria Cristina, ill. II. Title.

PS3562.E9465A6 2014

811'.54—dc23   2013 04116

First Edition   9 8 7 6 5 4 3 2 1

EVERYTHING IS A POEM

The Best of
J. Patrick Lewis

with illustrations by
Maria Cristina Pritelli

Creative Editions

TABLE OF CONTENTS

Foreword by J. Patrick Lewis   6

ANIMALS

Elephant Bill & Jackrabbit Jack (1987)   8
Fireflies (1986)   10
How the Yellow Jacket Lost Her Shyness (1992)   11
Midnight Blue, or The Cockroach's Song (1992)   12
Mosquito (1985)   14
One Cow, Two Moos (1985)   15
Ocean Diners (1982)   16
Snake Song (1986)   17
A Tomcat Is (1986)   18

PEOPLE

Baby Contralto (1994)   20
The Trumpeter (1996)   21
The First American Woman in Space (1990)   22
The First Human To Go Over Niagara Falls in a Barrel
   —and Survive (1993)   23
The First Man to Run a Four-Minute Mile (1988)   24
The Biggest Bubble-Gum Bubble Ever Blown (1997)   25
First Men on the Moon (1986)   26
The Greatest (1991)   28
I Decided ... to Stay Up in the Air Forever (1993)   29
The Many and the Few (1993)   31

READING

A Book Is (2001)   32
A Classic (2001)   33
The Gentleman Bookworm (1995)   34
Please Bury Me in the Library (2001)   36
Great, Good, Bad (1995)   38
Read ... Think ... Dream (1991)   39

SPORTS

Baseball Poem (2004)   40
How the Book of Baseball Was Written (2005)   41
The Kentucky Derby (1994)   42
The Longest Home Run (2005)   43
My Baseball Glove (2004)   44

RIDDLES AND EPITAPHS

Riddles (1993–2006)	46
Tombstone Poems (2002–2005)	52
A Dairy Farmer (2003)	52
A Baseball Pitcher (2005)	53
A Gardener (2002)	53
A Schoolteacher (2002)	53

MOTHER NATURE

The First Recorded 6,000-Year-Old Tree in America (1999)	54
The Gray of Day (2004)	57
Her-i-Cane (1995)	59
Nature's Art Gallery (2010)	60
Orange Johnson (1994)	63
What a Day (2010)	65
Weather, by the Old Masters (2010)	66

PLACES

What to Wear Where (1995)	68
Home Sweet Home (1995)	69
Okefenokee Swamp Song (1992)	70
Slowly around the U.S.A. (1992)	72
New Names, Old Places (1998)	73

A MIX

Are Bluebirds Why Houses Have Windows? (2003)	74
In the Middle of Your Face (1995)	76
Jump-Rope Rhyme (1997)	77
Postcard Poem (1996)	78
Say, Hay, Won't You Be Mine? (1995)	79
The Queen Takes Drawing Lessons (1995)	80
The Tablespoon Gallops Away (1993)	82
Under the Kissletoe (2003)	83
The Very, Very Finicky Queen of Trouble (1996)	84
Why Santa Sometimes Prefers the Front Door (2003)	86
Everything Is a Poem (2010)	87

What's the difference between a poem and a poem for children? That question has been debated for several centuries. The great poet Robert Frost once said that a poem "begins in delight and ends in wisdom." Another wordsmith, John Barr, a good friend who is also the former director of the Poetry Foundation, wrote that "a children's poem begins in delight and ends in ... more delight."

Of the definitions of poetry, there is no end. Elsewhere I have called poetry frosted fire, the tunnel at the end of the light, the nurse at the birth of the alphabet, a ladder to the castle in the air, a blind date with enchantment, and the sound of silence ... amplified. Whatever it is, poetry's key unlocks that strangest of all worlds: your imagination.

I was an unlucky fellow in that I did not discover poetry until I was just barely on the sunny side of forty. Then, having taught college economics for thirty years, I realized that I was in the wrong field with the wrong grasshoppers. You see, in my elementary school years, no teacher or librarian—or Pied Piper "Author's Day" writer—pointed me in the direction of word magic.

So I became—*ah-hem*—an opsimath. That is, one who learned late in life.

Once Sister Poetry grabbed me by the hand, it didn't take long to become a fool for verse. I hardly knew what to do with myself! I started out by sitting at the feet of two poets in particular. Edward Lear and Lewis Carroll were the best children's poets of the nineteenth century. Their work has endured—for good reason—and their books became my constant companions.

After nearly four years of reading classic poems and children's poems, rhymed and free verse, the great poets and the not-so-great (even the truly awful!), I thought I had learned the craft well enough to strike out on my own. So I said goodbye to my college students and began cobbling words together at the poet's trade in hopes of making a living.

As often happens, one week followed another, and before I knew it, seven years had passed. The one word I heard that whole time was NO! Rejections flew into my mailbox like mad Frisbees. And there were days, I admit, when I thought seriously about giving up and becoming a pianist, a glassblower, or somebody's Dutch uncle! But I kept telling myself what I have told children at the nearly five hundred author visits I have made around the world: *Nothing succeeds like failure*. Embrace failure; make it your friend. I fail a dozen times every day, and that's just before lunch!

One day, about thirty years ago, the swallows dared, and I received an acceptance. A publisher in New York had said YES to my first manuscript. I thought I felt a butterfly doing the salsa on my heart.

Although I have never taken a creative writing class, many writers have told me the first lesson they learned: Find your own voice. I suppose that's good advice, but not for me. I wanted to write poems in a hundred voices. That's why I decided to explore everything under and over the sun in as

many different ways as it's possible to write poetry. The kindest thing anyone has ever said about my work is how different it is from one poem to the next. If someone tells me, *I read a poem the other day, and I just knew that you had written it*, I appreciate the thought, but it doesn't reach my ears as a compliment.

Why not? Because the poem is always more important than the poet.

This is why you'll find many voices in my poems on subjects like extraordinary women, famous monuments, African Americans, extinct animals, weird holidays, twins (I'm one!), the Civil War, Galileo, Michelangelo, math and science, airplanes, underwear salesmen, riddles, rebuses, shape poems, anagrams, nonsense poetry, and every sort of wordplay. Some of my poems are gathered here in yet another exquisite Creative Editions book.

If you picked up *Everything Is a Poem* to be better educated, you're in for a disappointment. I wrote these poems to do nothing more or less than entertain the reader—to help unlock imaginations.

Have I succeeded? I don't know. Turn the page. You decide.

J. Patrick Lewis
March 2014

ELEPHANT BILL & JACKRABBIT JACK

Did you ever hear about Elephant Bill?
He tramped Elephant grass on Elephant Hill.
He had Elephant ears and an Elephant nose,
And Elephant wrinkles in his Elephant clothes.

Early one morning with the sun on his back,
Old Elephant Bill met Jackrabbit Jack,
Who had Jackrabbit fur and Jackrabbit teeth
And Jackrabbit jumpers tucked underneath.

Said Jackrabbit Jack to Elephant Bill,
"Let's race to the bottom of Elephant Hill,
Then race back up so that people can see
The mountain that ought to be named after *me*!"

Elephant Bill gave an Elephant laugh,
He beat Jack downhill by a mile and a half!
But they got to the bottom and had just
    turned around
When Elephant Bill heard a terrible sound—

The sound that an Elephant never forgets,
Jackrabbit had turned on his back-jumper jets!
And huffing below, old Elephant Bill
Looked up to the top of ... *Jackrabbit* Hill.

1987

FIREFLIES

An August night—
　The wind not quite
A wind, the sky
　Not just a sky—
And everywhere
　The speckled air
Of summer stars
　Alive in jars.

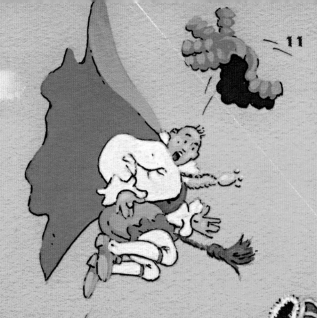

HOW THE YELLOW JACKET LOST HER SHYNESS

The King of England
Once was stung
Upon his royal bottom,
And you could hear
A yellow jacket
Yell, "Oh, boy, I got him!"

And that is how the yellow jacket
Finally lost her shyness,
And how the English
Came to call the King
"His Royal *High*ness!"

1992

MIDNIGHT BLUE,

My mama's name was Nightmare,
My daddy's name was Tricks.
And I was born outside a place called
Blueberry Muffin Mix.

I'm a cockroach from New Jersey,
And they call me Midnight Blue.
Free and easy living's what I do.
I'll get up to get me a late-night drink,
Cool my heels at the kitchen sink,
And before you know it, this old nose'll
Have me down the garbage disposal—
Easy living's what I do.

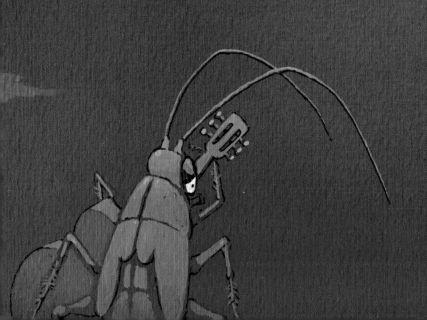

OR THE COCKROACH'S SONG

Well, I joined the Roaches' Union,
And I pay my union dues.
I obey the Cockroach Motto:
NEVER SLEEP IN HUMAN SHOES!
But I terrified a plumber once
And I musta spooked a kid
'Cause I got this reputation
For the creepy things I did.

I'm a cockroach from New Jersey,
And they call me Midnight Blue.
Don't know why folks keep on bawling
Every time they see me crawling....
Cockroach got to come a-calling,
Easy living's what I do.

MOSQUITO

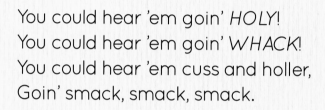

I was climbing up the sliding board
When suddenly I felt
A mosquito bite my bottom
And it raised a big red welt.

So I said to that mosquito,
"I'm sure you wouldn't mind
If I took a pair of tweezers
And I tweezered *your* behind!"
He shriveled up his body
And he shuffled to his feet,
And he said, "I'm awfully sorry
But mosquitos got to eat!
Still, there are mosquito manners,
And I must have just forgot 'em.
And I swear I'll never never never
Bite another bottom."

But a minute later Archie Hill
And Buck and Theo Brown
Were horsing on the monkey bars,
Hanging upside down.
They must have looked delicious
From mosquito's point of view
'Cause he bit 'em on the bottoms,
Archie, Buck, and Theo too!

You could hear 'em goin' *HOLY*!
You could hear 'em goin' *WHACK*!
You could hear 'em cuss and holler,
Goin' smack, smack, smack.

A mosquito's awful sneaky,
A mosquito's mighty sly,
But I never never never
Thought mosquito'd tell a lie.

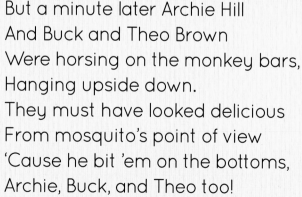

1985

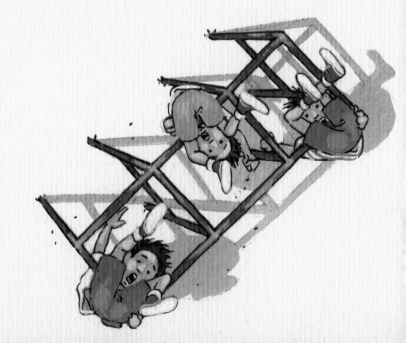

ONE COW, TWO MOOS

We used to have a single cow,
We called her Mrs. Rupple.
But she got struck by a lightning bolt,
And now we have a couple.

She's walking sort of funny now
Oh pity her poor calf.
Old Mrs. Rupple gives no milk.
She gives us half-and-half.

1985

OCEAN DINERS

They open up their beaks and throats
For breakfast off the backs of boats.

Some take a dip and dive for brunch,
Some join the passengers for lunch—

Or swoop in low for sneak attacks
On peanut butter & jelly snacks.

And when they're in a hungry mood,
Seagulls love your finger food!

1982

SNAKE SONG

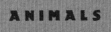

Toad gots measles
Frog gots mumps
Both gots such
Disgusting bumps.

They so ugly
It's a sin.
They be jumpin'
Out that skin.

Pay no mind
These creepy items
Close my eyes
I bite 'ems, bite 'ems.

A TOMCAT IS

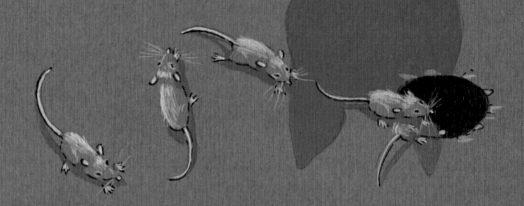

Nightwatchman of corners
Caretaker of naps
Leg-wrestler of pillows
Depresser of laps.

A master at whining
And dining on mouse
Designer of shadows
That hide in the house.

The bird-watching bandit
On needle-point claws
The chief of detectives
On marshmallow paws.

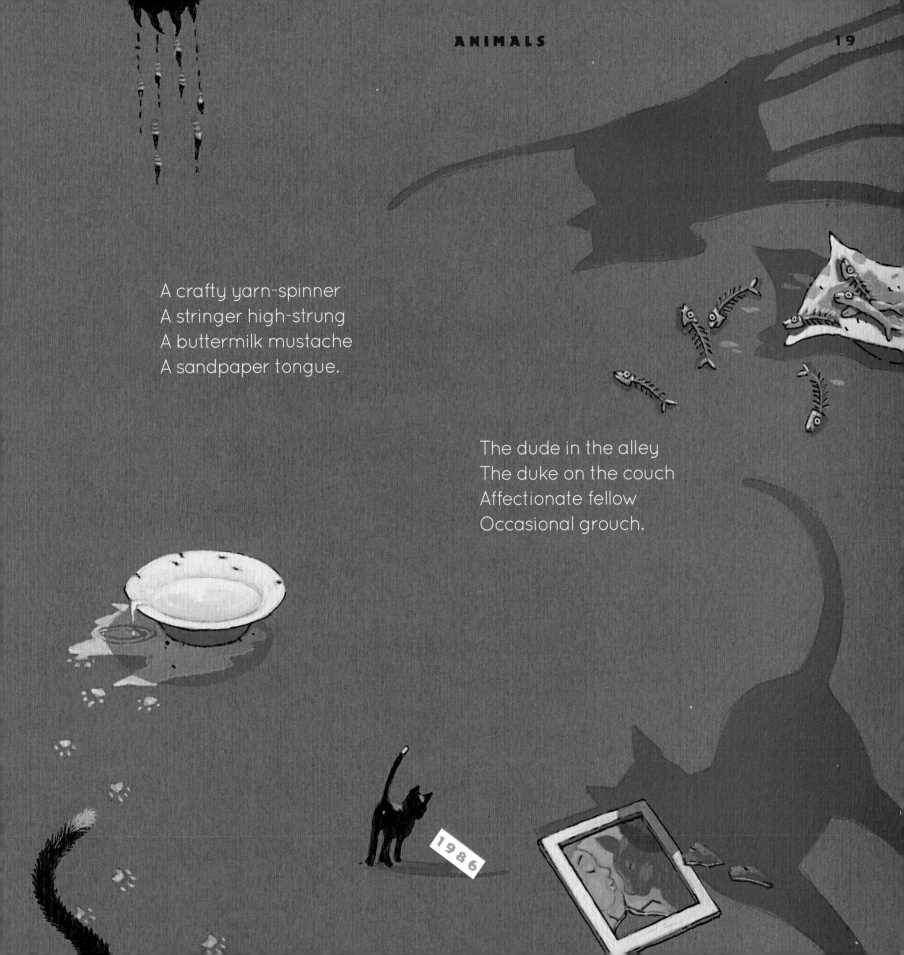

A crafty yarn-spinner
A stringer high-strung
A buttermilk mustache
A sandpaper tongue.

The dude in the alley
The duke on the couch
Affectionate fellow
Occasional grouch.

1986

BABY CONTRALTO

She brushed
Her voice
      Across the air
In colors
Not seen
      Anywhere.

In colors
Beautiful
      And strong,
She brushed
The air ...
      And painted song.

Marian Anderson / Singer / 1897-1993

1994

THE TRUMPETER

I am the trumpet   golden horn of plenty

I am the cat who   put kink in kookachoo

I am to tempo   what midnight is to mischief

I am the color   that dazzles <u>Kind of Blue</u>.

I am the fashion   a horn born into fusion,

I am painstaking   aching Mister Toot

I am the sounder   of solo Bye Bye Blackbird

I am in silence   a miser with a mute

I am the captain   too lucky with my sidemen

I am a combo   bebopper, pop and jazz

I am the thunder   arrives before the lightning

I am the whimper   that bluesy music has

Miles Davis / 1926–1991

1996

Sally K. Ride / 1951–2012 / First space flight on June 18, 1983

THE FIRST AMERICAN
WOMAN IN SPACE

Sally Ride rode
An alley-wide road
Into the sky.

Sally Ride road
To an area code
A million miles high.

Sally ride rode
With a precious payload
Out of Earthsight.

Sally Ride rode
Sally Ride Road
Into the night.

THE FIRST HUMAN TO GO OVER NIAGARA FALLS IN A BARREL—AND SURVIVE

How many dare-
Devils had tried
Niagara Falls?
How many died

Before a woman,
Forty-three,
Set out to test
The powers that be.

Her wooden barrel,
Set adrift
Above the Falls,
Soon met the swift

White-crested waves
Where others, brief-
Ly pitched and tossed,
Had come to grief.

And like a bobber
Far from shore,
Her barrel plunged
Across the roar

Of History.
In mist and steam,
Her little house
Was swept downstream.

The rescue party
Was amazed
To find the daring
Woman dazed,

But still alive!
What did she say?
How blessed I am
To see the day.

1993

Anna Edson Taylor / Horseshoe Falls / October 24, 1901

THE FIRST MAN TO RUN A FOUR-MINUTE MILE

Though Oxford clouds undid the day—
A chill kept many fans away—
The "dream mile" was a splendid race!
Young Brasher set the early pace
By going out extremely fast.
His teammates knew he wouldn't last,
And Chataway took the lead, as planned,
Just as they passed the viewing stand.
The half? 1:58.2!
At every curve the promise grew
That this day might be destiny.

And Roger Bannister knew that he
Could leap into the future, so
With some three hundred yards to go,
Began his kick, his head rolled back,
Pounding to glory down the track.
His body honed to perfect shape,
He won, collapsing at the tape!
And gave the credit to a team
That chased a boy who chased a dream.
He said, as history would tell,
"I did one thing supremely well."

Roger Bannister / Oxford, England / May 6, 1954 / 3:59.4 minutes

1988

THE BIGGEST BUBBLE-GUM BUBBLE EVER BLOWN

Susan Montgomery Williams one day
Had nothing to do when she went out to play,
So she took out some gum
And she started to chew
And to chew and to chew
Like a panda bear munching
A stalk of bamboo!

But Susan Montgomery
Williams just knew
If she blew and she blew
And she blew and she blew,
She'd pop the world gum-blowing
Record in two!

The bubble? It grew
And it grew and it grew
Until it had grown a foot wide,
And then ... *two*!

And now there's a girl
With her name in **Who's Who**!
(It's under Montgomery Williams—
That's Sue.)

23 inches wide / Fresno, CA / July 19, 1994

1997

FIRST MEN ON THE MOON

That afternoon in mid-July,
Two pilgrims watched from distant space
The Moon ballooning in the sky.
They rose to meet it face to face.

Their spidery spaceship *Eagle* dropped
Down gently on the lunar sand.
And when the module's engines stopped,
Cold silence fell across the land.

The first man down the ladder, Neil,
Spoke words that we remember now—
"Small step for man...." It made us feel
As if we too were there somehow.

When Neil planted the flag and Buzz
Collected lunar rocks and dust,
They hopped like kangaroos because
of gravity ... or wanderlust.

A quarter million miles away,
One small blue planet watched in awe.
And no one who was there that day
Will soon forget the Moon they saw.

1986

"The Eagle has landed!" / Apollo 11 Commander Neil A. Armstrong   "A magnificent desolation!" / Air Force Colonel Edwin E. "Buzz" Aldrin Jr. / July 20, 1969

THE GREATEST

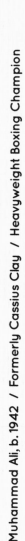
Muhammad Ali, b.1942 / Formerly Cassius Clay / Heavyweight Boxing Champion

His magic kingdom was the ring,
His secret weapon was the heart.
He took in stride and in full swing
Bewildered men he picked apart.

It wasn't just the flashy grin,
The fight promotion free-for-all:
He said before each bout he'd win
And then predict the round they'd fall.

The justly famous rope-a-dopes—
Pure wizardry casting a spell—
Were meant to raise then dash all hopes
Of men destroyed before the bell.

The world agreed on nothing much
But this one shouted word, Ali,
Three letters that conveyed, as such,
The virtue of tenacity.

He changed his name and took to God,
And he refused to go to war,
This fighting man of peace. How odd.
They do not make them anymore.

1991

Jesse Owens / Track Star and Olympic Gold Medalist / 1913–1980

I DECIDED ...
TO STAY UP IN THE AIR FOREVER

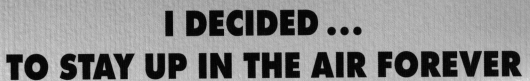

In 1936 Adolf Hitler sat
in his new Olympics Stadium,
eating a Bratwurst and sweating destiny.
110,000 fans waited for the Games
to begin when something happened
he could not bear to watch.
Onto the track stepped the world's
fastest human, who was not Aryan.
Not white.

Not worthy.
Not welcome.
The *Fuhrer* looked away without seeing
the man jump over Germany,
jump beyond hope and gravity,
beyond the dreams of ordinary people,
farther than any human would jump
for the next twenty-four years.

1993

THE MANY AND THE FEW

It was an Alabama day
For both the Many and the Few.
There wasn't really much to do;
No one had very much to say

Until a bus, the 6:15,
Drove by. But no one chanced
    to see
It stop to pick up history.
The doors closed slowly on a
    scene:

The quiet seamstress paid her
    fare
And took the one seat she could
    find,
And, as it happened, just behind
The Many People sitting there.

The Many People paid no mind
Until the driver, J. P. Blake,
Told the Few of *them* to take
The deeper seats. But she
    declined.

Blake stopped the bus and
    called police;
And Many a fire was set that night,
And Many a head turned
    ghostly white
Because she dared disturb the
    peace.

To celebrate the ride that marks
The debt the Many owe the Few,
That day of freedom grew into
The Century of Rosa Parks.

Rosa Parks / Civil Rights Activist / 1913–2005

1993

A BOOK IS

A whole in your pocket
A hitchhiker's guide
A road to time travel
A ticket to ride

A bundle of wonder
A mystery unsolved
(In which you will soon
Be directly involved)

A windfall in lap-land
A bedside surprise
A serving of sun
Under rain-wrecked skies

Rarely a lemon
But lemon meringue
The big enchilada
The whole shebang

2001

A CLASSIC

A children's book's a classic if
At six, excitedly,
You read it to another kid
Who just turned sixty-three.

2001

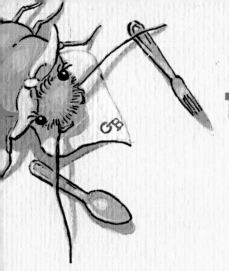

THE GENTLEMAN BOOKWORM

There once was a Gentleman Bookworm
Ate his words with a fork and a spoon.
    When friends crawled down
    From Book End Town,
He offered them *Goodnight Moon*.

He fed them *The Wind in the Willows*
And a page out of *Charlotte's Web*.
    They were eating bizarre
    Where the Wild Things Are,
When one of the guest worms said,

"How sinfully rich and delicious!
Why should anyone bother to cook?
    You've done it, dear boy!
    Now sit down and enjoy
A bit of a bite of a book!"

Having dined at the Table of Contents,
A worm, wiggling up to the host,
    Said, "When do we eat?"
    "Ah, *bon appetit*!"
Cried the Gentleman Bookworm. "A toast!

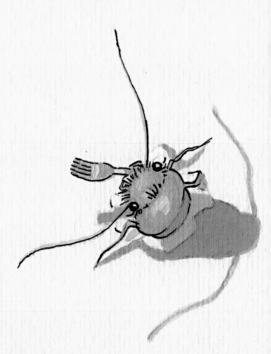

"Here's a bowl of my favorite verses
And a dish of ridiculous rhyme.
        But might I suggest,"
        Said the host to the guest,
"Chew them slowly. One line at a time."

So the worm waved her postage-stamp napkin.
Curled up in a little round ball,
        She proceeded to swallow
        The poems that follow
Until she had swallowed them all.

When the Gentleman's potluck had ended,
Not a poem-crumb littered the floor,
        And the worms who were able
        Crawled down from the table.
The host met his guests at the door.

"Please remember," he said as they wiggled
Home to book nooks and paperback racks,
        "It's especially wise
        To combine exercise
With a bowl full of poetry snacks!"

"Oh, what fun!" cried the gaggle of guest worms,
Who were laughing so hard that they shook.
        Then the giggling gourmet
        Up and wiggled away ...
And dove into a poetry book!

1995

PLEASE BURY ME IN THE LIBRARY

Please bury me in the library
In the clean, well-lighted stacks
Of Novels, History, Poetry
Right next to the Paperbacks,

Where the Kids' Books dance
With True Romance
And the Dictionary dozes.
Please bury me in the library
With a dozen long-stemmed proses

Way back by a rack of Magazines.
I won't be sad too often,
If they bury me in the library
With Bookworms in my coffin.

GREAT, GOOD, BAD

A great book is a homing device
for navigating paradise.

A good book somehow makes you care
about the comfort of a chair.

A bad book owes to many trees
a forest of apologies.

READ ... THINK ... DREAM

Book me a passage
    to history
Back to some once-
    on-a-time,
Sail me into a
    tall-told tale,
Read me a river-
    boat rhyme.

Ride me the waves
    of a story,
Settle me down
    by a brook,
Dream me a land
    only dreamed of,
Book me a voyage
    by book.

1991

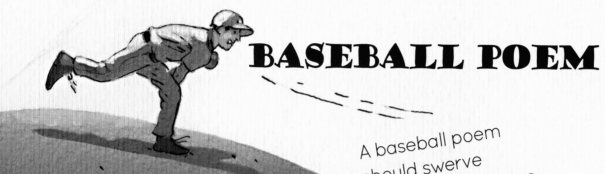

BASEBALL POEM

A baseball poem
should swerve
like a sidearm curve

or tease a designated reader
with sublime

off-rhyme.

A baseball poem
should be as unexpected, say,
as an undetected
squeeze play

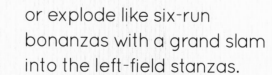

or explode like six-run
bonanzas with a grand slam
into the left-field stanzas.

2004

HOW THE BOOK OF BASEBALL WAS WRITTEN

An old man who lived alone on an island
was a little sad. Sprayed by whitecaps,
swayed by trade winds, he had only
his daybook, a pen, and a young boy's heart
for company. Each day the sun rode out
at noon.

One morning a word—gleaming and new,
never heard before—appeared like the glint
of a ship's hull on a distant swell.
He watched a gull pose, holding up the sky,
a tortoise grip the earth as if it were
a carousel. The new word hung in the air
until he reached out—and caught it.

Shortstop.

The old man put it down
in his daybook,
and kept on writing.

2005

THE KENTUCKY DERBY

Hugging the clubhouse turn,
Whipping along the rail,
The wind at Churchill Downs
Picks up the pace to sail

With Whirlaway, Citation,
Gallant Fox, Seattle Slew,
Swaps or Secretariat.
The pack comes into view,

And as they turn for home
Four-leggeds feel the crack-
ing whip hand of the wind
Racing around the track,

But let the records show,
Of all the Triple Crowns,
The wind has never won
A Place at Churchill Downs.

1994

THE LONGEST HOME RUN

was longer than
the Wright brothers flew in 15 seconds,
two Statues of Liberty,
three Goodyear blimps,
the width of four football fields,
five Douglas firs,
six blue whales,
seven Diplodocuses
or nine Great Sphinxes!

Your pick.

The Mick

Mickey Mantle / New York Yankees / 643 feet / September 10, 1960 / Briggs Stadium, Detroit

MY BASEBALL GLOVE

My friend walks in
To see the prize,
Regret and envy
In his eyes.

Its leather cracks
In places where
Sure hits once died
Without a prayer

And baseballs, bored
With being caught,
Left seams that seem
An afterthought.

Though weather's worn
Its perfect shape,
Remembered now
With packing tape,

My glove knows how
It used to be
And stretches out
To sleep with me.

2004

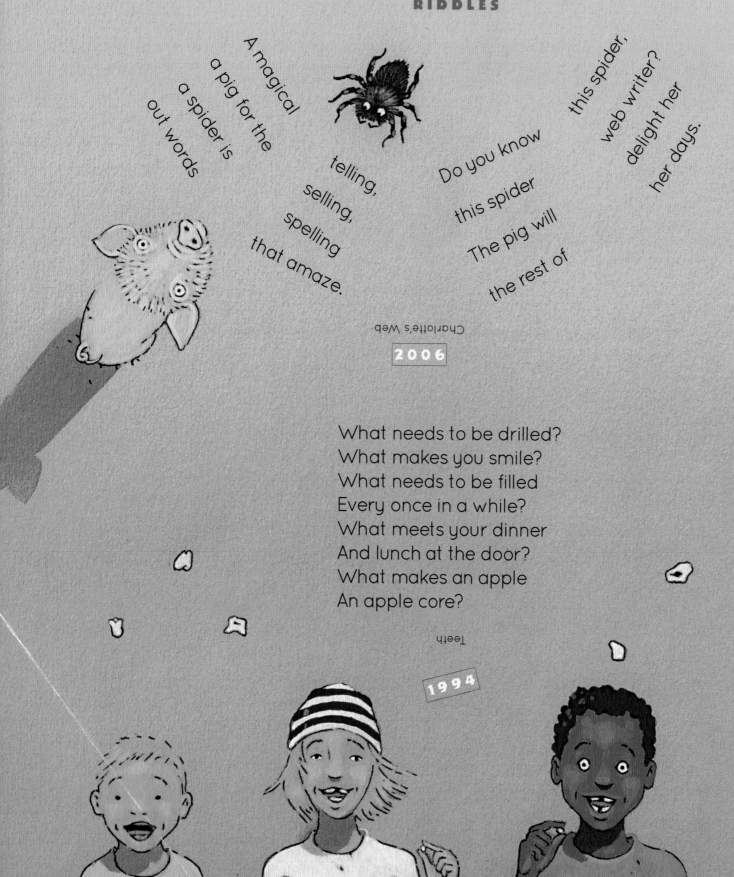

A magical
a pig for the
a spider is
out words

telling,
selling,
spelling
that amaze.

Do you know
this spider
The pig will
the rest of

this spider,
web writer?
delight her
her days.

Charlotte's Web

2006

What needs to be drilled?
What makes you smile?
What needs to be filled
Every once in a while?
What meets your dinner
And lunch at the door?
What makes an apple
An apple core?

Teeth

1994

Imagine a castle
without any towers,
or a thundercloud bursting
without any showers.
Now imagine a bull
who loved only flowers.

One day he went wild.
(The cause: a bee sting!)
So they brought him to fight
matadors in the ring.
Instead he sat smelling
the flowers of spring.

You can't make a bull
always follow the herd.
The very idea is
completely absurd.

Ferdinand the Bull

To folks in Maine
   They're red and round,
And you can find them
   Underground.

In Idaho
   They're brown and big,
But still grow under-
   Ground. You dig?

Potato

After the heavy traffic of rain,
The sun gives a green light
To a truck of colors making
A U-turn in the sky.

A Rainbow

1994

1995

As I was driving to Van Nuys,
I met a hangman who had three eyes.
Bloodshot the one—it stopped me cold.
The second blinked a shocking gold.
But when the third turned green as grass,
The three-eyed hangman let me pass.

A Traffic Light

1995

The middle of a table
The end of a tub
In front of a battleship
In back of a sub
A bus to start off with
A cab at the end
I hope you will be my
B-you-tiful friend.

The Letter B

Which tree can hang
    Along a lake,
Whose branches bend
    But will not break,
Whose leaves, sun-summered
    Into bloom,
Can whisk the water
    Like a broom?
Which tree will sigh
    As ripples pass
Across the crystal
    Looking glass,
Then lean beyond
    The shore's long shelf,
Reflecting sadly
    On itself?

A Weeping Willow

1994

I am you
but bigger than you
and longer than you
and darker than you

You are me
but smaller than me
and shorter than me
and scared of me

Your Shadow

1994

A Dairy Farmer
Here lies little Larry LaGow,
Who sat in the shade
Of his Galloway cow,
Tied up her tail
Behind a hind udder,
Filled a milk bucket
For Saturday's butter.
Flew off the stool,
Went down on his knees,
Coaxing his cow
For Sunday cream cheese.
Here is a lesson
For Larry LaGow.

NEVER SIT UNDER
A GALLOWAY COW.

2003

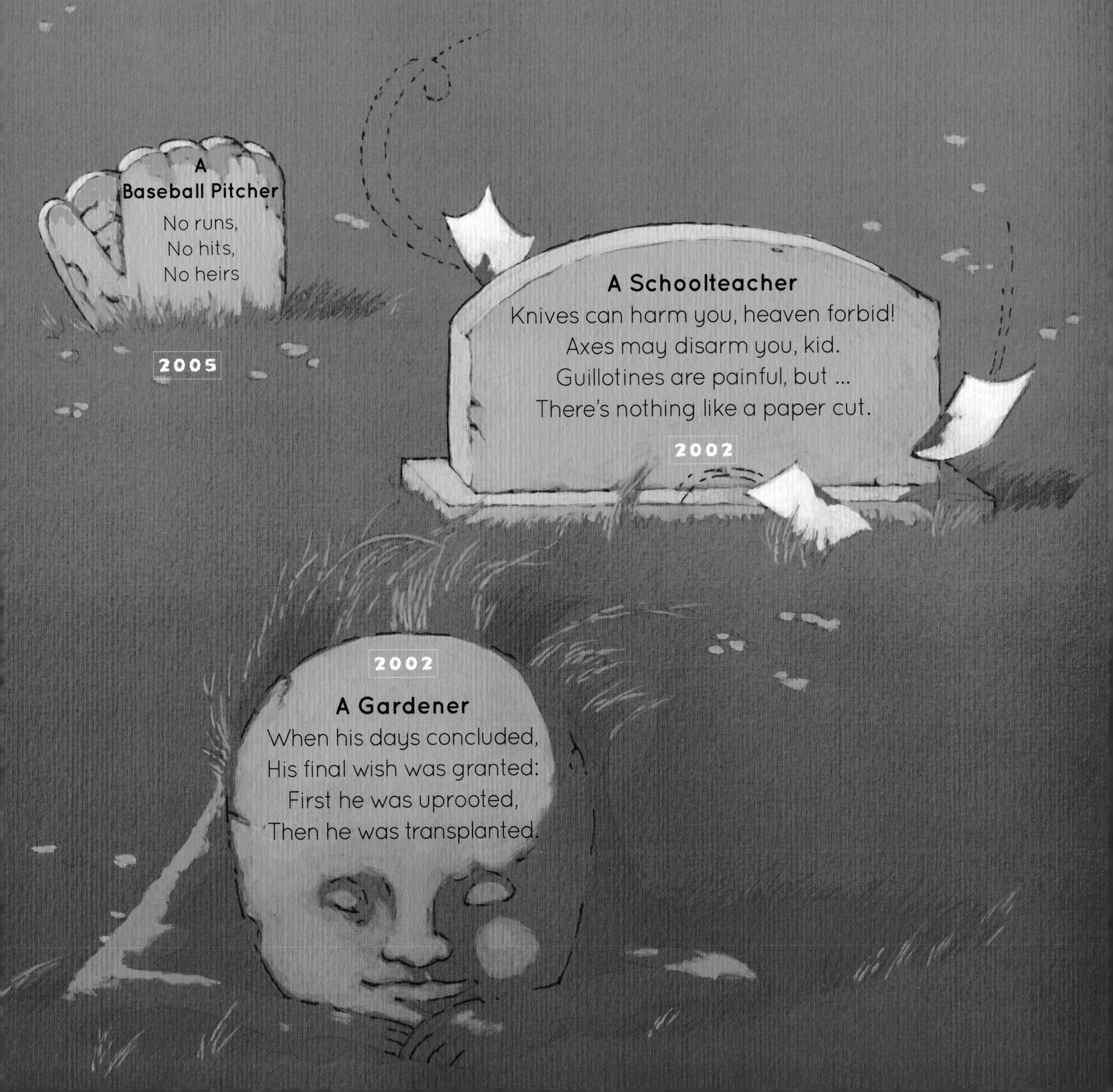

**A
Baseball Pitcher**

No runs,
No hits,
No heirs

2005

A Schoolteacher
Knives can harm you, heaven forbid!
Axes may disarm you, kid.
Guillotines are painful, but ...
There's nothing like a paper cut.

2002

2002

A Gardener
When his days concluded,
His final wish was granted:
First he was uprooted,
Then he was transplanted.

THE FIRST RECORDED 6,000-YEAR-OLD TREE IN AMERICA

When Mother Nature held her ground,
When almost no one was around,
A redwood bud began to grow
And watch the seasons come and go.

For sixty centuries or more,
It stood upon the forest floor
And waved its arms about the sky
And sang a sea breeze lullaby.

December 1977:
The Eon Tree, so tall to heaven,
Bowed gracefully and bid farewell
To all its fellow trees,
                    and fell.

1999

The "Eon Tree" / A coast redwood / Humboldt County, CA / 250 feet tall, about 6,200 years old

THE GRAY OF DAY

Shy Evening paints all heaven gray,
Erasing blue from balmy Day,

Uncolors brute box elders, oaks,
And elms with even, gentle strokes,

Then finds the houses, whereupon
She dabs her brush ... their lights come on

As if two dozen stars fell down
To twinkle life into the town.

But Evening's easel leaves undone
One mischief streak of western Sun

To grace the masterpiece she drew—
Still Life: An Evening's Point of View—

Till he robs her of fading light,
That thief of art, black-hearted Night.

HER-I-CANE

There was a curly her-i-cane,
Her name was Lorelei.
And all she ever wanted was
    To fly, fly, fly.

She wasn't like the other girls,
For Lori never grew
Into a proper her-i-cane
    That flew, flew, flew.

She twisted round the ocean.
She meant to touch the sky.
It took her tiny breath away
    To try, try, try.

So Lorelei decided
To a gentle wind be true—
She breezed right into autumn
    And she blew, blew, blew.

1995

NATURE'S ART GALLERY

Wind's paintbrush strokes in streaks the trees.
It knows without
being
told
this miracle,
ages
old—
Novembering
maples
gold.

2010

ORANGE JOHNSON

Orange Johnson
   Wakes at dawn,
Puts his golden
   Slippers on,
Climbs the summer
   Sky at noon,
Trading places
   With the moon.

Orange Johnson
   Runs away
With the blue
   Tag end of day,
Switching off the
   Globe lamplight,
Pulling down
   The shades of night.

1994

WHAT A DAY

Out of dark's rougher neighborhoods,

Morning stumbles,

none too

bright,

recalling now

the thief,

Night,

who stole her work

2010

of art—

Light.

WEATHER,
BY THE OLD MASTERS

The Michelangelo thunder
of an April
cloudburst
hints
at what follows
a great
rinse:
spring meadows in
Monet
prints.

WHAT TO WEAR WHERE

When I was a boy
In Looziana,
We wore blue jeans
And a red bandanna.

My folks moved up
To the state of Maine,
We wore duck shoes
In slicker-suit rain.

My folks moved down
To the state of Texas,
We wore brand names
Like Lazy X's.

Now that we're living
It up in Vermont,
We wear pretty much
Whatever we want.

HOME SWEET HOME

I met my wife in Houdy, Miss.
Or was it Odear, Me.?
We bought a house in Fiven, Tenn.
And lived so happily.

But then we moved to Shapeless, Mass.,
From there to Reeley, Ill.
And ended up in Sayno, Mo.,
Where folks keep mighty still.

1995

OKEFENOKEE SWAMP SONG

Southern Georgia/Northern Florida

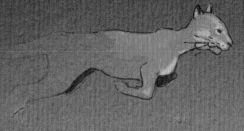

The panthers run
And the alligators sun
Themselves in the Okefenokee,
Where the cypress smoke
And the frogs go croaking
Down in the Okefenokee.

Down in the black-brown watery town
Known as the Okefenokee.
Down in the black-brown watery town
Known as the Okefenokee.

A National Park
So thick and dark
The dogs step backward just to bark
Down in the Okefenokee.
From longleaf pine
Drips turpentine,
And folks sure love to monkeyshine
Down in the Okefenokee.

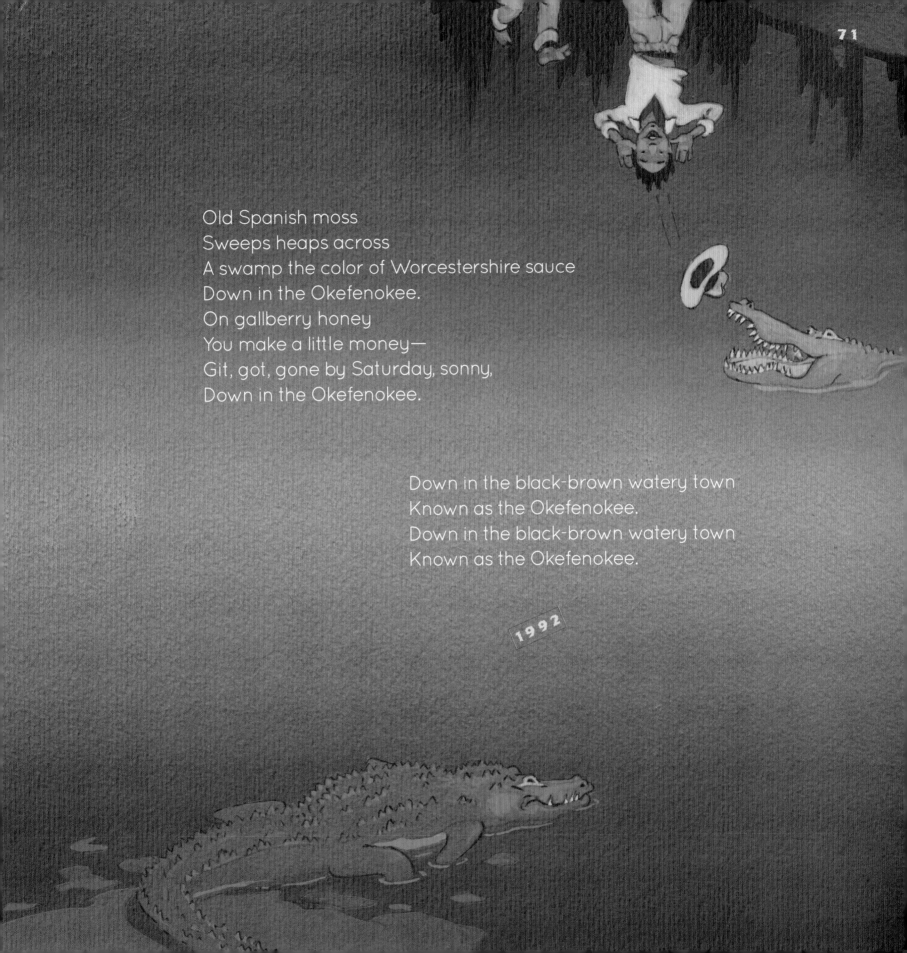

Old Spanish moss
Sweeps heaps across
A swamp the color of Worcestershire sauce
Down in the Okefenokee.
On gallberry honey
You make a little money—
Git, got, gone by Saturday, sonny,
Down in the Okefenokee.

Down in the black-brown watery town
Known as the Okefenokee.
Down in the black-brown watery town
Known as the Okefenokee.

1992

SLOWLY AROUND THE U.S.A.

If I had nothing else to do ...,

I'd write a birthday card to you
But send it off to someone who,
Say, lived in Millinocket, Maine,
And very carefully explain
That she should quickly mail it on
By way of Portland, Oregon,
And when it got there they would know
To forward it to Buffalo,
New York, so that the person there
Would have to send it first class air
To Boston, Mass. and back again
By overnight delivery.

Then, from Nashville, Tennessee to Knox-
Ville, c/o of Auntie's P.O. Box,
So she could zip it Fed Express
To your Chicago, Ill. address.
And someday, maybe mid-July—
A birthday card!—you'd wonder why
It took so long to get to you!
I'd call you up and tell you, too ...,

If I had nothing else to do.

1992

NEW NAMES, OLD PLACES

Sri Lanka used to be **Ceylon**.
Ancient **Persia**? Now **Iran**.

Zaire was **Congo** way back when,
Now it's **Congo** once again.

China? Can you guess? **Cathay**.
That's what people used to say.

Thailand once was known as **Siam**.
Gold Coast turned to **Ghana**. I am

Always interested in telling
How a country changed its spelling.

Dutch East Indies? **Indonesia**!
Once **Zimbabwe** was **Rhodesia**.

Burma changed to **Myanmar**.
Russia, once **USSR**,

Was even earlier called **Rus'**.
Other countries introduce

Brand new names occasionally.
Can *you* find one or two ... or three?

1998

ARE BLUEBIRDS WHY HOUSES HAVE WINDOWS?

Is sadness
the reason
for rainbows?

Are gardens
why people
have knees?

Are bluebirds
why houses
have windows?

Are geese
the inventors
of V's?

A drought is
the rain's
inspiration.

A flood
is a river's
despair.

The sun
is a storm
on vacation.

A rose
is a gift
to the air.

The sky's
a high-fashion
designer.

The ocean's
a bowl of
fish soup.

Blue whale
was the first
ocean liner.

And sea gulls
made up the
word *swoop*.

Snowflakes
are the world's
art collection.

A full moon's
a firefly to
the stars.

A canyon's
a flatland's
correction.

The wind's
just a gust
of guitars.

Would tides
like to skip
daily practice

At filling
the shore's
hourglass?

Are porcupines
cousins
to cactus?

Are jellyfish
breakable
glass?

An orchard's
the reason
for ladders.

The tallest
trees laugh
at a stair.

A weed is
indeed a
misunderstood
seed.

But a rose,
oh a rose,
always wins
by a nose,
a rose is a gift
to the air.

2003

Do you often take for granted
Something that is squarely planted
Sometimes straight but mostly slanted
In the middle of your face?

Think how often you'd surprise
Neighbors with your flat disguise
If nothing separates your eyes
In the middle of your face.

IN THE MIDDLE OF YOUR FACE

It's impossible to speak
(Or dance alone, yes, cheek-to-cheek)
If there is nothing left to tweak
In the middle of your face.

So be grateful for your nose
Because it's just where it's supposed
To be for taking all those blows
In the middle of your face.

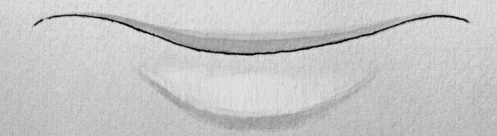

1995

JUMP-ROPE RHYME

Feet that feel good fly

Toes that feel good tap

Hands that feel good clap

Fingers that feel good snap

Arms that feel good swing

Lungs that feel good sing

Heels that feel good click

Legs that feel good kick

Eyes that feel good wink

Heads that feel good think

Feet that feel good fly

Off the ground. Good-bye!

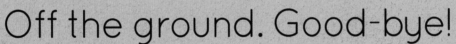

POSTCARD POEM

Find yourself a quarter
Buy yourself a stamp
Tap it on your tongue
Until it's damp damp damp
Stick on a postcard
Mail it to a friend
Tell her you will be one
Till the end end end

SAY, HAY, WON'T YOU BE MINE?

If you were the last brown bale of hay
And I were a melon vine,
I might just creep on up to you—
  Say, hay, won't you be mine?

If you were a husk of Indian corn
And I were a bolder crow,
We'd wait for Grandma Frost to dust
  This meadow white with snow.

If you were a thousand columbines
And I were your long cool drink,
A charm of hummingbirds could spend
  All summer here, I think.

1995

THE QUEEN
TAKES DRAWING LESSONS

For Edward Lear

At Buckingham Palace in royal red
    The Queen of England drew
A portrait of herself, and said,
    "Now tell me, tell me true!"
Her Lords began to weep because
Each knew exactly <u>what</u> it was
    But none of them knew <u>who</u>!

The first one cried, "Beef Stroganoff!"
    The second said, "Hyena?"
The third exclaimed, "It's slightly off
    The Coast of Argentina!"
The more they wept, the more they guessed—
    "Potatoes in their skin?"
"A Tuning Fork!" "A Buzzard's Nest!"
    "The Duke of Wellington?"

"You nincompoops!" the royal jaw
     Shot back, and cracked the chandelier.
"I'll have you know I learned to draw
     From Master Mr. Lear.
Go fetch the famous lad for me!"
Her Lords looked up. "Your Majesty,
     He's standing in the rear."

As Lear approached the Head of State,
     He saw that quirk of art
And thought of ... Beef upon a Plate?!
     It nearly broke his heart.
But all he said was, "Ah, my Queen?"
     And fell into her lap
As large and lean as the Argentine.
     She smiled. "You clevah chap!"

1995

THE TABLESPOON GALLOPS AWAY

In Oneida, New York,
Live a Knife and a Fork
And a pip of a Tablespoon.

Whenever he passes
The Waterford glasses,
The Tablespoon tinkles a tune.

Knife and Fork sit at supper
With beautiful Tupper-
Ware bowls full of spinach souffle.

While the Tablespoon gallops
Away with the scallops,
And cries, "Hi-ho, Silver! Away!"

1993

UNDER THE KISSLETOE

A miss'll know
To kiss hello—

The kiss'll go
With mistletoe.

The miss'll glow
For this'll show

That bliss'll grow
From kissletoe.

2003

THE VERY, VERY FINICKY QUEEN OF TROUBLE

The Town of Trouble couldn't count
The troubles they had seen
Because of all the pouting
By Her Majesty, the Queen.

She pouted from the parlor,
Kitchen, garden, balconies,
At weddings and at funerals
And on anniversaries.

One evening as she pitter-
Pattered round the Royal Loft,
She cried, "The Royal Mattress
Is too hard, or else too soft!

1996

"Is it too much to request—
After all I am the Queen—
That I'd like a little rest
On a bed that's in between?"

And so it was that I stepped forth
To say what I would do.
"I'm Isabella Abnormella
Pinkerton McPugh."

"Excuse me, Isabella Abnormella,
Uhh, McWho?"
The King could not believe his ears,
"And who, pray tell, are you?"

"I'm Keeper of the Royal Cat,
Your Royal Highness, sir,
And I'll invent a Royal Cot
To make Her Highness purr."

I had a funny gunny sack
Sewn forty times as large
And filled with water from the moat
(I put the King in charge).

And the ending to this story,
As the history books have said,
Was the wonderful invention of ...
The Queen-sized water bed!

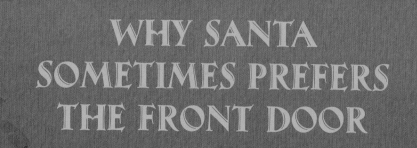

WHY SANTA
SOMETIMES PREFERS
THE FRONT DOOR

He remembers
Those Decembers
Burning embers,
Chimney holes,

When he splendid-
ly descended,
But rear-ended ...
On the coals!

2003

EVERYTHING IS A POEM

A garden is a poem
Lined with rows of similes
Like lyrical chrysanthemums
And epic peonies.

A spider web's a poem
Composed upon the air,
Silk-designed and deftly lined
To catch the unaware.

A mirror is a poem
Revealing truths about
The poet, but it often leaves
The shadow of a doubt.

A firefly's a poem,
A flashy verse sublime
That's read by other fireflies
One sparkle at a time.

A picture is a poem
If it's painted in disguise
On a canvas of emotion
From a palette of surprise.

A rainbow is a poem,
A phenomenon so rare,
It's not that it is written
But is written on the air.

A shining star's a poem
Penned by ghostwriter, the
Moon,
Who publishes her verses
In a book called *Clair de Lune*.

A busy bee's a poem
With nectar that's so fine
A reader-eater laps up every
Honey of a line.

2010

CREATIVE EDITIONS BOOKS BY J. PATRICK LEWIS

Everything Is a Poem: The Best of J. Patrick Lewis. 2014. Art by Maria Cristina Pritelli.

Harlem Hellfighters. 2014. Art by Gary Kelley.

The Good Ship Crocodile. 2013. Art by Monique Felix.

Self-Portrait with Seven Fingers: The Life of Marc Chagall in Verse.

(With Jane Yolen.) 2011. Reproductions of original art of Marc Chagall.

And the Soldiers Sang. 2011. Art by Gary Kelley.

Skywriting: Poems to Fly. 2010. Art by Laszlo Kubinyi.

The House. 2009. Art by Roberto Innocenti.

Michelangelo's World. 2007. Original art; cover by Etienne Delessert.

Black Cat Bone. 2006. Art by Gary Kelley.

VHERSES: A Celebration of Outstanding Women. 2005. Art by Mark Summers.

The Stolen Smile. 2004. Art by Gary Kelley.

Galileo's Universe. 2003. Art by Tom Curry.

Swan Song. 2003. Art by Christopher Wormell.

The Last Resort. 2002. Art by Roberto Innocenti.

The Shoe Tree of Chagrin. 2001. Art by Chris Sheban.

Freedom Like Sunlight. 2000. Art by John Thompson.

BoshBlobberBosh. 1998. Art by Gary Kelley.